MY FAVORITE DOG

SHETLAND SHEEPDOGS

by Rhonda E. Nichols

Kaleidoscope
Minneapolis, MN

The Quest for Discovery Never Ends

· ·

This edition first published in 2022 by Kaleidoscope Publishing, Inc.

No part of this publication may be reproduced in whole or in part without written permission of the publisher.

For information regarding permission, write to Kaleidoscope Publishing, Inc.
6012 Blue Circle Drive
Minnetonka, MN 55343

Library of Congress Control Number
2021934867

ISBN
978-1-64519-470-5 (library bound)
978-1-64519-478-1 (ebook)

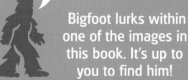

Bigfoot lurks within one of the images in this book. It's up to you to find him!

TABLE OF
CONTENTS

Ready? Go!

"Almost ready, Lola!" Emma says as she sets up a hurdle. She puts tables together to make a tunnel, hangs a hoop from a tree, and sets up poles in a line. "Done!" Emma has turned her backyard into an **agility** course. Lola is a Shetland Sheepdog. They're known for being world-class competitors in agility. Emma has been practicing with Lola for fun.

"Come, Lola," Emma calls. Lola runs over and excitedly spins in circles. Emma can't wait for her parents to see Lola complete the course. They cheer as she and Lola stand at the starting line. "Ready, Lola?" she asks. Lola barks. Emma gets ready to run. "Go!"

Chapter 1

The Story of Shetland Sheepdogs

A Shetland Sheepdog stands alert. It's his job to keep the Shetland ponies safe. A young pony gallops too far from the group. The Shetland Sheepdog acts quickly. He sprints around the pony and gives a sharp bark. Startled, the pony turns back.

"Good boy," the farmer praises. Sometimes there was too little food on the Shetland Islands in Scotland. Animals needed to be small so they would eat less. That's why farmers had ponies, not horses. The farmers needed a dog who could herd ponies and live in cold weather. Collies from the Scottish **mainland** were the perfect dogs for this job. They were bred to be smaller, and the Shetland Sheepdog was born!

A CHANGE IN NAME

Shetland Sheepdogs use to be called
Shetland Collies. Collie fans didn't like this.
They made the Kennel Club in England
change the name to Shetland Sheepdogs
in the early 1900s.

Not all Shetland Sheepdogs live on Shetland Island anymore, but most of them used to. People who lived on the mainland didn't know Shetland Sheepdogs existed until the early 1900s. People rarely visited because it's hard to get to the islands.

Shetland Sheepdogs are still known as herders. Dog breeds are put into groups. Shetland Sheepdogs are in the Herding Group. Dogs in this group have an **instinct** to gather, herd, and protect other animals. Other breeds in this group include Border Collies, German Shepherd Dogs, and Pembroke Welsh Corgis.

A Border Collie

A German Shepherd

A Pembroke Welsh Corgi

Some Shetland Sheepdogs still herd animals, but they also perform other jobs and sports now. They work as therapy dogs or compete in **obedience**, agility, herding, or tracking events. Like Lola, Shetland Sheepdogs are very quick, smart, and obedient.

Where **SHETLAND SHEEPDOGS** come from

 COUNTRY OF ORIGIN

Shetland Islands, Scotland

Atlantic Ocean

SCOTLAND

North Sea

UNITED KINGDOM

IRELAND

ENGLAND

Chapter 2

Looking at a Shetland Sheepdog

A sable Shetland Sheepdog

Lola jumps over the hurdle. Her long fur flies about. Shetland Sheepdogs can have many different colored coats. They can have blue merle coats, which have gray smears and spots.

A bi-black Shetland Sheepdog

A blue merle Shetland Sheepdog

A tricolor Shetland Sheepdog

Shetland Sheepdogs can also have sable coats. A sable coat has a mix of brownish-red and yellow fur and black and gray fur. They can also have all-black fur, or a mix of colors. Most Shetland Sheepdogs have white markings on their faces, necks, chests, undersides, legs, and tips of their tails.

A bi-blue Shetland Sheepdog

SHETLAND SHEEPDOG

MALES AND FEMALES

HEIGHT:*
13-16 inches (33-41 cm)

WEIGHT:
15-25 pounds (6.8-11 kg)

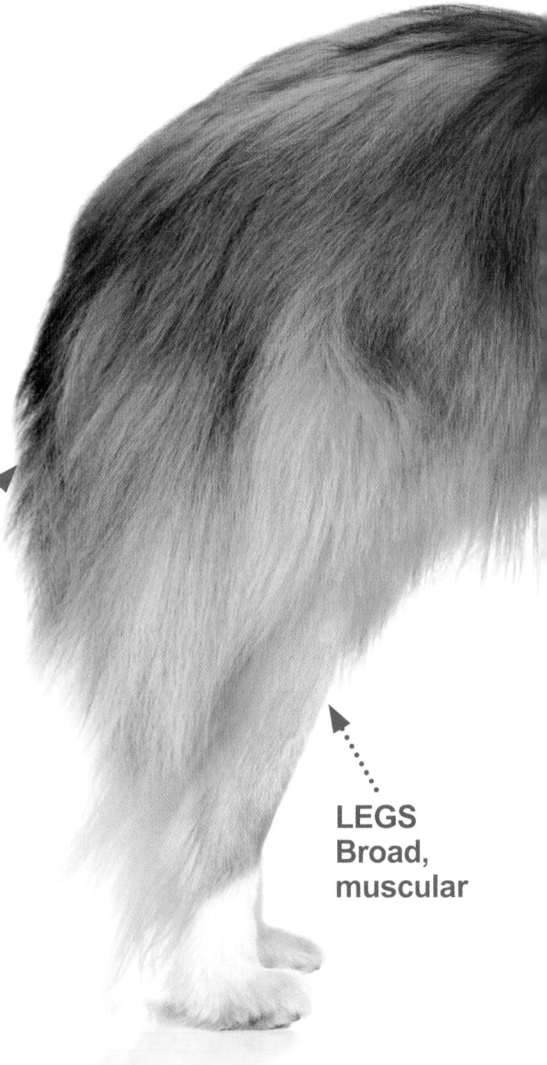

TAIL
Long

LEGS
Broad,
muscular

*The height of a dog is measured
from the top of the shoulder, not
from the top of the head.

HEAD
Long

EARS
Small, high on
head, tips fall
forward

EYES
Almond-
shaped,
gentle

COAT
Long, straight,
harsh; undercoat
is short and thick

PAWS
Oval, compact,
tough pads,
strong nails

"Tunnel!" Emma runs by the tables. Lola sprints under them. Shetland Sheepdogs may be small, but they're strong! Emma can see how they would

be able to keep up with ponies.
The poles are next on the obstacle course.

"Weave!" Emma commands. With her quick paws, Lola zigzags through the poles. It's time for the hoop! Emma hopes Lola can make it. It'd be a perfect run! "Hoop!" Lola jumps. And she makes it! They cross the finish line as her parents cheer for them. "Good girl, Lola!" Emma hugs her and gives her a treat. It was hard work to train Lola, but it felt more like play because they had so much fun together.

Chapter 3

Meet a Shetland Sheepdog!

Lola trots over to Emma's parents. They pet her and give her praise. She turns in happy circles. Emma is proud of her little pup. She remembers when she first met Lola. It took Lola time to warm up to her.

WATCHDOG ON THE JOB

Shetland Sheepdogs were bred to watch over and protect animals. If they sensed danger, they barked to let their farmers know. Today, Shetland Sheepdogs like Lola that don't live on farms are great at telling their owners when someone is at the door.

Like other Shetland Sheepdogs, Lola is **wary** of strangers. Shetland Sheepdogs usually don't trust new people. This makes them great watchdogs.

Lola bounds over to Emma and runs in circles. "Yes, you did a good job!" Emma praises. "But will you help me clean up?" Lola rolls onto her back for tummy scratches. Emma laughs. "Worth a shot." She loves how Lola grew to trust and love her. Shetland Sheepdogs are affectionate when they learn to trust a person.

FUN FACT

Sometimes Shetland Sheepdogs will herd children into a group.

Emma takes Lola to the dog park every evening. Lola is quick to bark a friendly hello to people she remembers. And she's always ready to play with her friends.

Shetland Sheepdogs are often called "Shelties." They use to be called "Toonie Dogs." "Toon" is a Shetland word meaning farm.

Chapter 4

Caring for a Shetland Sheepdog

Shetland Sheepdogs have a lot of fur. This makes them super fluffy. But it also makes them shed a lot. After their walk, Emma grabs a brush. She brushes Lola's long overcoat and also her short undercoat. Lola wags her tail. She loves to have clean fur, especially after a day of running the obstacle course.

Shetland Sheepdogs were bred to be active. Emma makes sure Lola gets plenty of exercise.

Emma is almost done brushing Lola's fur. She checks behind Lola's ears. If there are any mats, or big knots, of fur, Emma needs to brush them out so Lola can stay healthy. Emma also checks the elbows of her front legs and her pants, which is the long fur under her tail.

FUN FACT

Shetland Sheepdogs don't need to bathe very often unless they're dirty from playing outside.

It's dinnertime and Lola knows it! She circles Emma and guides her to her bowl with a bark. "Stop herding me, Lola," Emma laughs. She gives her a scoop of food. The **veterinarian** recommended a high-quality dog food that has the right **nutrients** for Lola's age. Even when Lola gives Emma puppy eyes, Emma doesn't give her more food. She doesn't want to overfeed her.

TREAT THEM WITH KINDNESS

Do you want to teach your dog a new trick? Choose a healthy treat. Dogs love treats, but don't give them too many! When your dog does something you like, reward your dog with kind words or a treat. If your dog does something you don't like, ignore the behavior. This is called positive training.

After dinner, Emma gently scrubs Lola's teeth with a toothbrush. Dogs need their teeth brushed just like humans do. Emma uses a dog toothpaste. Human toothpaste would make Lola sick. "All clean!"

Emma gives Lola a scratch between her ears and climbs into bed.

"Up!" she says. Just like in the obstacle course, Lola obeys and jumps onto the bed. "Good girl, Lola." Emma can't wait to practice more tricks tomorrow. Maybe she'll teach Lola to climb up a ramp like in the agility competitions. Emma pets Lola's long, clean fur as they fall asleep. She can't believe how lucky she is to have such a sweet and smart dog.

THINK

FIND OUT MORE. There is so much more to dig up about Shetland Sheepdogs. What do you want to learn? Find out more on the American Kennel Club website. Or look for a Shetland Sheepdog club in your area. You can meet people who love them as much as you do!

CREATE

ART TIME. Can you draw a Shetland Sheepdog? Look up a cute picture and grab some markers and paper. Will your pup have a fancy hairstyle? Will it wear a fun hat? What is its favorite toy or game? Does it have a job? The sky is the limit!

SHARE

THE MORE WHO KNOW. Share what you learned about Shetland Sheepdogs. Use your own words to write a paragraph. What are the main ideas of this book? What facts from the book can you use to support those ideas? Share your paragraph with a classmate. Do they have any comments or questions about Shetland Sheepdogs?

GROW

HELP OUT! There are dogs near you that need care. Animal shelters can be great places to volunteer and hang out with pups. Contact a shelter near you and find out if you can help. Or can your family donate food or gear to help rescue dogs? Find out why dogs end up in shelters. Is there anything you can do to help them find homes?

RESEARCH NINJA

Visit *www.ninjaresearcher.com/4705* to learn how
to take your research skills and book report writing to the next level!

Research

SEARCH LIKE A PRO
Learn how to use search engines to find useful websites.

FACT OR FAKE
Discover how you can tell a trusted website from an untrustworthy resource.

TEXT DETECTIVE
Explore how to zero in on the information you need most.

SHOW YOUR WORK
Research responsibly—learn how to cite sources.

Write

GET TO THE POINT
Learn how to express your main ideas.

PLAN OF ATTACK
Learn prewriting exercises and create an outline.

Further Resources

BOOKS

Gagne, Tammy. *Collies, Corgis, and Other Herding Dogs*. North Mankato, Minn.: Capstone Publishing, 2017.

Leaf, Christina. *Awesome Dogs: Shetland Sheepdogs*. Minnetonka, Minn.: Bellwether Media, Inc., 2017.

Rosen, Michael J. *A Dog's Life: Speaking to Your Dog*. Mankato, Minn.: The Creative Company, 2019.

WEBSITES

FACTSURFER

Factsurfer.com gives you a safe, fun way to find more information.

1. Go to www.factsurfer.com.

2. Enter "Shetland Sheepdogs" into the search box and click 🔍

3. Select your book cover to see a list of related websites.

Glossary

agility: the ability to move quickly and easily.

instinct: a habit an animal or person is born with.

mainland: the main part of land in a country; not an island.

nutrients: the right kind of food to stay healthy and grow.

obedience: listening to a command. Obedience trials test how well a dog listens to its handler.

undercoat: the first layer of fur on an animal.

veterinarian: a doctor for animals.

wary: being careful in case there could be danger.

Index

PHOTO CREDITS

About the Author

Rhonda E. Nichols is a budding author. She loves to write about animals and all of their wonderful characteristics and survival techniques. Nichols has written narrative nonfiction series about animals of the deep, high fliers, and many more creatures, including man's best friend. Her best friend isn't a dog, though. It's an African dwarf frog named Max!